Bridges

Written by
Etta Kaner

Illustrated by
Pat Cupples

Kids Can Press

To my budding engineers: Yael and Ora

ACKNOWLEDGEMENTS

I am grateful to the following people for giving so generously of their time and knowledge during the writing of this book. Thank you to Roland Bergmann of Yolles Partnership Ltd. and Roger Dorton of the Ministry of Transportation of Ontario for their patient and clear bridge engineering explanations as well as their careful review of the manuscript; Geoff Day of the City of York Board of Education for his valuable suggestions; Peter Leach at Algoma Steel Inc. for information about the use of steel in bridge building; Dael E. Morris of the Royal Ontario Museum for her information about army ants; Dr. Timothy Myles of the University of Toronto for his fascinating details about subterranean termites; Ranjit Reel of the Ministry of Transportation of Ontario for engineering details; Laurie Wark, my editor at Kids Can Press, for her usual insight, encouragement and good humour; writer and friend Frieda Wishinsky for her clever suggestions; and to my family, who patiently built bridges and created riddles with me.

Kids Can Press acknowledges the financial support of the Ontario Arts Council, the Canada Council for the Arts and the Government of Canada, through the BPIDP, for our publishing activity.

Published in Canada by
Kids Can Press Ltd.
29 Birch Avenue
Toronto, ON M4V 1E2

Published in the U.S. by
Kids Can Press Ltd.
4500 Witmer Estates
Niagara Falls, NY 14305-1386

Edited by Laurie Wark
Designed by Esperança Melo
Printed and bound in Canada

CM 94 0 9 8 7 6 5 4 3

Canadian Cataloguing in Publication Data

Kaner, Etta
    Bridges

ISBN 1-55074-146-2

1. Bridges — Juvenile literature. 2. Bridges — Design and construction — Juvenile literature. 3. Bridges — Models — Juvenile literature. 4. Handicraft — Juvenile literature.
I. Cupples, Patricia. II. Title.

TG148.K35 1994   j624.2   C94-930092-6

Kids Can Press is a Nelvana company

CONTENTS

INTRODUCTION

Hello. I'm Jan Lapont. I'm an engineer. You've probably driven over or under some of the many bridges my team and I have designed. We have built bridges over rivers and lakes, highways and roads, ravines and railway tracks. Each one of our bridges is different from the other.

Simple beam bridges, like the one being built here, cross city roads and highways. Cantilever truss bridges, like the Quebec Bridge, carry railroad tracks. Graceful arch bridges, like the Sydney Harbour Bridge, span deep harbours or steep gorges. Delicate-looking yet strong suspension bridges, like the Humber Estuary Bridge, are built to cross very wide waterways. There are even moveable bridges, like the famous Tower Bridge.

Before we design a bridge, we investigate the site where the bridge is to be built. We need to know how long the bridge should be and if the ground is strong enough to support a bridge. Will the bridge carry heavy trains, or will large ships pass under it? How much traffic will there be on the bridge? What are the wind and weather conditions like?

Once we have gathered this information, we decide what kind of bridge to build. Our architect helps design a bridge that will be suitable for the conditions and pleasing to look at. He makes sure that the bridge is designed to fit into its surroundings.

In this book you will become part of the bridge-building team. You'll come across some of the problems that engineers face and

4

discover for yourself how to solve them. By building models of bridges and testing them for strength, you will find out the secret of using certain shapes in bridges and why some materials work better than others.

All you need are an engineer's notepad, to keep track of your discoveries, and some building materials that you can probably find around home. Make a notepad by stapling some papers together at the top. Whenever you see this sign you might want to use the notepad. So put on your hard hat and let's get building!

If you find a bridge word that you do not understand, check the glossary on page 46 for an explanation.

Q. What card game do engineers like to play?

A. Bridge.

I'm a geo-technical engineer, or soil expert. I drill deep holes into the ground where a bridge is going to be built. From these holes I take samples of soil and rock, which tell us if the earth is strong enough to support a bridge. Then we know what kind of foundation to use.

I'm the architect of the team. I draw diagrams that show how the bridge will look when it is finished. Jan and I decide what kinds of materials are best to use.

1. Beam Bridges

Have you ever crossed a stream by walking along a log? Then you have used a beam bridge. In fact, this was probably the first kind of bridge ever built by humans, thousands of years ago. People still build beam bridges. The bridges today are longer and are built out of concrete or steel instead of logs. And, just as a log is supported at its ends by the banks of the stream, the beam of a modern beam bridge must also be supported. The beam, or roadway, is supported by land at either end, by tall columns called piers or by both. A beam bridge over a road or highway often is not very long or high, but its roadway, or beam, must still be strong enough to support a lot of weight.

Build a Beam Bridge

Before a bridge is built, engineers sometimes make models of bridges and test them for strength. Make some models of beam bridges and find out what kinds of beams are strong.

You'll need:
- Plasticine or other modelling material
- 2 bricks (or 2 blocks of wood or 2 equal piles of books)
- 10 or more strips of manilla tagboard (3-ply Bristol board), each 15 cm x 45 cm (6 inches x 18 inches)

1. Make ten or more balls of Plasticine, each about 2.5 cm (1 inch) across (a little smaller than a ping-pong ball). Each ball should be about the same weight. You might want to mould the balls into people or cars since they will be used to test your beam's strength.

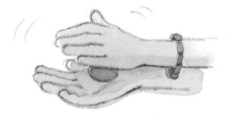

2. Stand the bricks upright 30 cm (12 inches) apart.

3. Lay one strip of tagboard across the bricks to form a beam bridge. How many balls of Plasticine does it hold?

4. Fold strips in different ways to make different kinds of beams. In your engineering notepad, record the number of balls each kind of beam holds. Here are a few ideas to get you started.

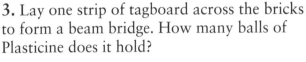

Which kind of beam was the strongest? Probably this one:

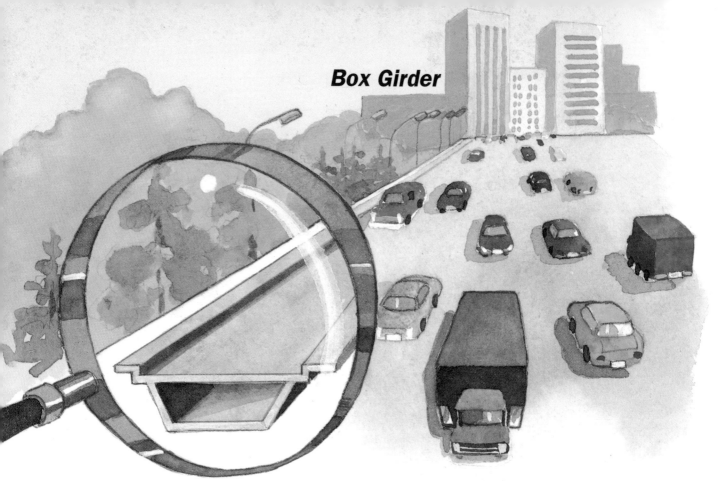

Box Girder

Engineers design beam bridges with long hollow boxes underneath the roadway, or deck, to give the bridge strength. These box girders run the full length of the bridge and are made of concrete or steel. They are light because they are hollow, yet strong because of their shape and stiffness.

Try building a beam bridge with box girders, and find out how strong they are.

You'll need:
- scissors
- 2 strips of manilla tagboard, each 15 cm x 45 cm (6 inches x 18 inches)
- glue
- 2 bricks (or 2 blocks of wood or 2 equal piles of books)
- Plasticine balls

1. Cut one of the strips of tagboard in half lengthwise to form two strips.

2. Fold each side of these two strips up 1 cm (1/2 inch) and then over again the same amount. Open the sides as shown.

3. Glue the two folded strips to one side of the untouched strip of tagboard.

4. Stand the bricks upright and lay the beam across them. Test the beam for strength with your Plasticine balls.

How many Plasticine balls does the box-girder bridge hold? How does it compare to the accordion-fold beam? What happens when you test a beam built with more than two box girders?

A CITY OF BRIDGES

Can you guess which city has the most bridges in the world? It's Venice, Italy. Venice has 450 bridges spanning the canals that are the city's streets.

Two of these bridges are world-famous. They were both designed by the same architect — Antonio da Ponte — in the late 1500s. The Rialto Bridge is a beautifully decorated arch bridge lined with shops. The Bridge of Sighs has sculptured faces on it. Prisoners crossed it on their way to prison after they were sentenced.

Longer Beam Bridges

Simple beam bridges, like the ones you tested, are built across waterways or roads that are usually no wider than 30 m (100 feet). But what if you needed to build a longer beam bridge, like the Pontchartrain Causeway in Louisiana, U.S.A? It is so long (38 km [24 miles]) that you can't see any land when you stand in the middle of it.

There are two ways to build long beam bridges. One way is to build the roadway out of many short beams called spans. A span goes from one supporting column, or pier, to another. The spans are connected with joints made out of flexible material. The other way to build a longer beam bridge is to use longer beams and support them with as many piers

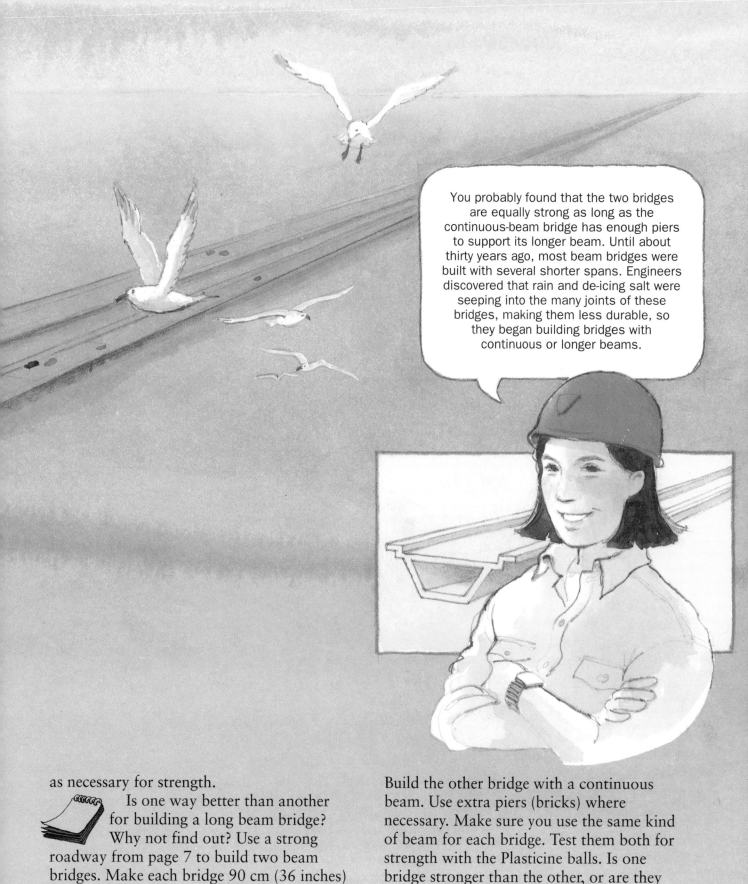

You probably found that the two bridges are equally strong as long as the continuous-beam bridge has enough piers to support its longer beam. Until about thirty years ago, most beam bridges were built with several shorter spans. Engineers discovered that rain and de-icing salt were seeping into the many joints of these bridges, making them less durable, so they began building bridges with continuous or longer beams.

as necessary for strength.

Is one way better than another for building a long beam bridge? Why not find out? Use a strong roadway from page 7 to build two beam bridges. Make each bridge 90 cm (36 inches) long. Build one bridge with two spans, each 45 cm (18 inches) long, attached with tape.

Build the other bridge with a continuous beam. Use extra piers (bricks) where necessary. Make sure you use the same kind of beam for each bridge. Test them both for strength with the Plasticine balls. Is one bridge stronger than the other, or are they both the same? What happens if you make the beams even longer?

11

Piers — Which Shape Is Best?

When you built your longer beam bridge, you needed several brick piers to support the roadway. Engineers use columns of concrete as piers to support beam bridges. To build piers on land, bridge builders use long plywood or steel moulds called formwork. The formwork is placed into a huge hole dug in the ground. Concrete is poured into the formwork, and after the concrete hardens, the formwork is removed, just as a mould is removed from jelly after the jelly has set. The roadway, or deck, is then fitted onto the piers.

As you drive under beam bridges, check out the shape of the piers that support those bridges. Are the piers shaped like triangles, cylinders or squares? Bridge builders use one of these shapes because it's the strongest. Try this experiment to find out which one it is.

You'll need:
- 3 sheets of paper, each 21 cm x 27 cm (8 1/2 inches x 11 inches)
- sticky tape
- a pile of paperback books

1. Fold one sheet of paper in half. Open it up.

2. Fold each side of the same sheet into the centre. Open it up.

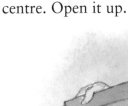

3. Tape the paper into a square column.

4. Fold another sheet into three equal parts. Open it up. Use the tape to make a triangular column.

5. Roll the third sheet into a cylinder with the ends slightly overlapping. Tape it closed.

6. Stand the three columns on their ends. Pile books one at a time onto each column. Make sure each book is balanced before you add the next one. Which shape holds the most books before collapsing?

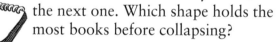

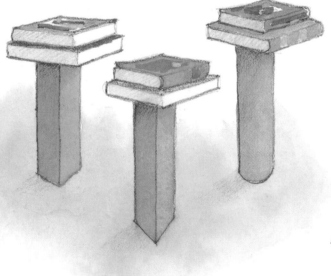

You probably found that the cylinder supports the most books. This shape is strongest for the piers of beam bridges, too. Since a cylinder has no corners, the weight of a roadway pressing down on it is spread out evenly all around. This helps the pier to resist buckling.

Q. What bridge can you never cross?

A. The bridge on your nose.

Bridge Materials

Today, bridges are built out of steel, concrete or a combination of both. Concrete is a mixture of water, sand, small stones and a grey powder called cement. Concrete is very strong when it is in compression, that is, when heavy loads press down on it. It sounds perfect for supporting heavy traffic, right? But concrete has one major problem. It is weak when in tension — when it's being stretched. Check this out for yourself.

Find a sponge at least 14 cm (5 1/2 inches) long. With a marker, draw vertical (up and down) lines 2 cm (3/4 inch) apart along one side of the sponge. Rest the ends of the sponge on bricks to make a bridge. Put a can of tuna on the sponge. What happens to the spaces between the lines on the side of the sponge? They are squeezed together (in compression) at the top. They are pulled wider (in tension) at the bottom. When this happens with a concrete beam, tiny tension cracks form along the bottom of the concrete. When heavy loads press on concrete beams, what happens? Put some more cans on your sponge bridge and find out. You got it. Eventually, the tension cracks in concrete beams become longer, and the beam collapses.

Can you make the sponge bridge stronger? Try using two knitting needles or two long sharp pencils. If you put the two knitting needles through the sponge lengthwise, how many cans of tuna will your sponge bridge support? To prevent concrete beams from cracking at the bottom, steel rods are put through them. This is called reinforced concrete.

The first example of reinforced concrete was found in a beam over the door of a Roman tomb built more than two thousand years ago. The beam was reinforced with bronze rods.

USE YOUR NOODLE

Next time you have spaghetti for supper, think about building a bridge with it. That's what competitors in the annual spaghetti bridge-building contest do in Kelowna, British Columbia. Contestants use glue and up to 750 g (about 3/4 of a bag) of uncooked spaghetti to build a bridge. The bridge must span 1 m (3 feet). Winning bridges have supported as much as 231 kg (509 pounds) — that's strong enough to hold three adults!

Cantilever Bridges

Try balancing a ruler on the edge of a table so that three-quarters of it extends beyond the edge of the table. It doesn't stay on the table, does it? What if you use some Plasticine balls to help you?

Congratulations! You have just figured out how a cantilever bridge works.

A real cantilever bridge has a beam coming out from each side of a river, where they are supported by concrete slabs, or abutments. The beams meet in the middle of the bridge. Sometimes there is a third span between them, to make the bridge longer. Each beam balances on a pier at its centre.

The longest cantilever bridge in the world is built exactly like this. The Quebec Bridge, which crosses the St. Lawrence River in Canada, has two steel arms, or cantilevers, balanced on piers with a centre section called a suspended span joining the cantilevers. The main span of the Quebec Bridge is 549 m (1801 feet). That's about as long as six football fields laid end to end.

Try building a cantilever bridge out of Lego or other building material. How long can you make it? How strong is it? You will probably need to build the piers and side supports, or abutments, first, before making the cantilevers that balance on the piers. It took 17 years to complete the Quebec Bridge. You should be able to build your cantilever bridge in a lot less time!

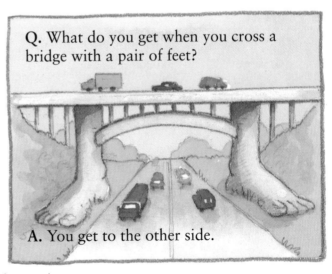

Q. What do you get when you cross a bridge with a pair of feet?

A. You get to the other side.

Covered Bridges

Many of the bridges that pioneers built looked like long wooden houses spanning a river. They built these covered bridges to protect the wooden roadway from rain, ice and snow. Some people called them kissing bridges because young couples would sneak kisses as they crossed the bridge in their horse-drawn buggy.

There are still hundreds of covered bridges in use around the world. The Hartland Bridge, which crosses the St. John River in New Brunswick, Canada, is the longest covered bridge in the world. It was built in 1899 and is about as long as four football fields laid end to end.

INSECT ENGINEERS

Subterranean termites (termites that live underground) have an amazing way of protecting their sensitive bodies from light when they travel above ground. The termites make tiny covered bridges called shelter tubes to travel through when exploring for dead wood. The shelter tubes are made of a paste of fine soil and saliva mixed in the termites' mouths. The tubes are about 1 cm (1/2 inch) wide and 3 cm (1 1/2 inches) high, and they can be as long as 10 m (yards). The tubes usually run up the sides of buildings or trees. Sometimes they are free-standing and look like thin telephone poles.

Truss Bridges

In the late 1800s, the train became a popular way to transport goods and people across North America. Bridge builders faced some new problems. They needed to create a bridge that would be strong enough to support the massive weight of trains, as well as to withstand the vibrations that moving trains create. Bridge builders found that a truss bridge did both these things.

Truss bridges are similar to beam bridges, but truss bridges use a pattern of geometrical shapes called trusses. These shapes are rigid — they don't move when pushed — and they make the bridge strong, especially when a heavy train is rumbling along it. Which shape is the most rigid — a square? a triangle? a rectangle? Why not find out for yourself?

You'll need:
- scissors
- 3 index cards, each 7.5 cm x 12.5 cm (3 inches x 5 inches)
- a single-hole punch
- 11 small paper fasteners

1. Cut the end off each index card so that it measures 7.5 cm x 10 cm (3 inches x 4 inches).

2. Cut each card in half lengthwise. Cut each half in half lengthwise again. You now have 12 strips, but you will need only 10.

3. Punch a hole in each end of the 10 strips.

4. Attach three strips with the paper fasteners to make a triangle.

5. Attach four strips to make a square.

6. Cut one strip in half widthwise. Punch a hole in the unpunched ends. Use these shorter pieces to make a rectangle with two longer strips.

7. Lay the triangle, square and rectangle on a table. Push on any two sides of each shape.

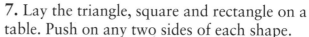

 Which shapes move or change shape? Can you add a longer strip to the square and rectangle so that they don't move? What shape have you made inside them? What shape is best to use when building a truss bridge?

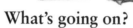

What's going on?

Truss bridges use triangles to give them strength. Triangles are used for the trusses at the sides and for the horizontal bracing of the bridge. Triangles can be organized into many patterns to make strong trusses. These patterns are named after the people who invented them.

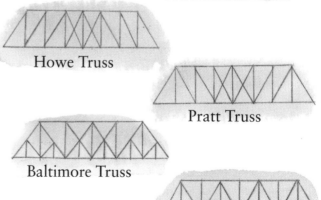

Town Lattice Truss

Howe Truss

Pratt Truss

Baltimore Truss

Warren Truss

19

Build a Truss Bridge

Can you build a truss bridge at least 60 cm (2 feet) long? Try to construct one that will support at least 12 balls of Plasticine.

You'll need:
- a piece of paper and a pencil
- scissors
- a package of index cards 7.5 cm x 12.5 cm (3 inches x 5 inches)
- a single-hole punch
- a box of paper fasteners
- a package of index cards 15 cm x 20 cm (6 inches x 8 inches)

1. Sketch a pattern of triangles that you would like to use for your bridge. You might want to start with a simple pattern, such as the one shown here, and change it as you go along.

2. To build a triangle, cut two smaller index cards in half lengthwise. Fold each half in half lengthwise.

3. Punch a hole in each end. Open each half so that it forms a right angle.

4. Attach three strips, or struts, with paper fasteners to form a triangle.

5. Join the two lines of triangles with struts across the top and bottom. You can use struts made with larger index cards to strengthen the squares formed at the top and bottom of your bridge.

Did you wonder why you used folded struts for your truss bridge, instead of simple strips? Check your engineering notes on testing beams for the answer (see page 9).

Problems with Steel

One of the most famous truss bridges was the Tay Bridge in Scotland. On a windy night, a year after it was completed, the bridge collapsed. Unfortunately, part of a passenger train crossing the bridge at the time fell into the water below, and many people died.

Why did the bridge collapse? Investigators found two reasons. The bridge had not been properly designed to resist strong winds, and rust had eaten through the iron piers and weakened them so much that the bridge collapsed under the weight of the train. How could this tragedy have been prevented? Try this experiment and find out.

You'll need:
- 2 steel nails
- 3 yogurt or margarine containers
- water
- a paintbrush
- house paint
- 1 galvanized steel nail

1. Place one steel nail in a container. Cover it with 5 cm (2 inches) of water.

2. Paint the other steel nail with two coats of paint. Let it dry. Place it in a container and cover it with water.

3. Place the galvanized steel nail in a container and cover it with water.

4. Leave all the nails in their containers. What changes do you see in the nails after one day? after two days? after ten days?

What's Going On?
You probably noticed that the steel nail in the first container rusted, just as the piers of the Tay Bridge did. That's because steel is made with iron, which rusts when it comes in contact with water and air. After several days, the painted nail probably showed some rust, too. The galvanized nail (coated with zinc) showed no rusting at all.

It might be a good idea to build bridges out of galvanized steel, but it would usually be too expensive. Today, some bridges are built with weathering steel, to reduce rusting. When weathering steel is exposed to air and water, it forms a coating of oxide on its surface. This oxide coating inhibits rusting and corrosion. Other bridges, such as the famous Forth Rail Bridge in Scotland, are painted with zinc and vinyl paint, to fight against rust. Painting such a large bridge is an endless job. By the time a team of workers finishes painting the whole bridge (it takes three years), the other end needs painting, and they have to start all over again.

2. Arch Bridges

How would you design a bridge that had to span a gorge as deep as a ten-storey building? Could piers that tall be strong enough to support a roadway? Yes, but they would be too expensive to build. Instead of a beam bridge, you could use an arch bridge.

For thousands of years, arch bridges were built of wedge-shaped stone blocks called voussoirs. The voussoirs were placed over the surface of a wooden arch-shaped framework that was first built across a gorge. The blocks were inserted against a middle block called the keystone. When all of the voussoirs were in place, the wooden arch was removed. The pressure of the blocks against the keystone held the arch up.

You can imitate the pressure of voussoirs against a keystone. Stand facing a friend with your arms outstretched towards each other. Grasp each other's hands, raise your arms to make an arch and lean towards each other. Can you feel the pressure on your hands? Your interlocked hands are acting as the keystone in an arch bridge.

22

Modern Arch Bridges

Today, arch bridges are constructed out of reinforced concrete or steel. Concrete arches can be built like stone arches, but instead of stones, huge hollow concrete blocks are used. Steel arch bridges are built by joining curved steel beams together. Starting at each end of the bridge, beams are added on until they meet in the middle. One of the most famous and widest steel arch bridges in the world is the Sydney Harbour Bridge in Australia. It is so wide that it can carry two railroad tracks, eight lanes of roadway, a bicycle path and a path for pedestrians.

ROMAN ARCHES

The Romans, who were expert engineers, always used semicircles for the arches on their bridges. A bridge spanning a wide river had many stone arches joined to one another, with piers in between. Often the number of arches was odd so that the middle arch could be wider than the side arches. This wide arch provided a larger space for boats to pass through and made the bridge more pleasing to the eye.

The most amazing arch bridges built by the Romans were aqueducts. Aqueducts were built about two thousand years ago to carry water across valleys and rivers to the many cities throughout the Roman Empire. The water ran in a channel at the top of several tiers of arches. The longest Roman aqueduct was the Aqueduct of Carthage in Tunisia. It was 141 km (88 miles) long and could carry 31.8 million L (7 million gallons) of water a day — that's enough water to fill 200 000 bathtubs. Can you imagine how many arches were needed for a bridge that size?

Building Arches

Bend a strip of manilla tagboard into an arch and place it on a table. Does it keep its shape? What can you do to make the tagboard keep its arch shape?

You could place something solid, such as books or bricks, at either end of the arch. Bridge builders do the same thing. They build huge abutments at each end of the arch to resist the thrusts created by the arches.

LONDON BRIDGE IS FALLING DOWN ...

You probably know the nursery rhyme "London Bridge Is Falling Down," but do you know why someone made it up?

The original London Bridge was made of wood. In the 11th century, a fleet of Norsemen led by King Olaf invaded England. They sailed up the Thames and tied ropes to the bridge's piers. Then they rowed downstream with all their might until the bridge collapsed. Some historians believe that the nursery rhyme was made up at that time.

The bridge was rebuilt and destroyed by fire a number of times, but finally it was built out of stone. This stone bridge lasted until 1968, when the London government decided to build a new London Bridge. Instead of destroying the old one, the government sold it to Lake Havasu City, in Arizona, U.S.A. How did they move 10 161 t (10 000 tons) of granite across the ocean? Before the bridge was taken apart, each block was numbered. When the blocks reached Arizona, they were put back together in the correct order, like a giant jigsaw puzzle.

Are All Arches the Same?

Arches can have different shapes. Is one shape stronger than another? Try this to find out.

You'll need:
- scissors
- 2 strips of manilla tagboard, each 15 cm x 45 cm (6 inches x 18 inches)
- a ruler
- some hardcover books of different sizes
- 10 balls of Plasticine

1. Cut one strip of tagboard so that it is 30 cm (12 inches) long.

2. On a table, use this strip to make an arch 20 cm (8 inches) wide. Use books to support the arch. The books should be as high as the arch.

3. Lay the other strip across the top of the books and the arch. This is the roadway of the bridge.

4. Test the strength of the arch by putting the Plasticine balls on the roadway one at a time.

5. Make other arch bridges with narrower spans: 18 cm (7 inches), 15 cm (6 inches), 12.5 cm (5 inches). Which bridge is the strongest?

Roadways on arch bridges run above, below or even through the arch. The road is connected to the arch by vertical struts, or bars, of different lengths. Can you connect your roadway to the arch with cardboard strips? Just make a right-angle fold at each end of the strips and glue the folded parts to the roadway and arch. Does that make a difference in the strength of the bridge?

3. Suspension Bridges

Suspension bridges are the best bridges to build over very large bodies of water. The strong steel ropes, or cables, that curve from one tall tower to the other easily support a very long roadway. But how do engineers get that first rope across from one side of the water to the other?

Charles Ellet solved this problem in a very unusual way. In 1850, when he was asked to build a suspension bridge across the gorge at Niagara Falls, Canada, he decided to hold a kite-flying contest. He offered five dollars to the first person to fly a kite across the 235-m-(770-foot-) wide gorge. A boy named Homan Walsh won the prize. His kite string was tied to a light steel wire that was tied to a heavier wire. Once the bridge builders tied the heavy wire to the other side of the gap, the cables of the suspension bridge could be built.

Build a Suspension Bridge

Why not try building your own suspension bridge? Don't worry; you won't have to fly a kite to get it started! First you'll construct the towers, cables and anchorages, then you'll build the roadway.

You'll need:
- 2 identical chairs
- thick string
- 4 bricks (or 4 heavy books)
- scissors
- a large cardboard carton
- packing tape

Building the towers, cables and anchorages

1. Place the chairs with their backs facing each other. The chairs are the bridge's towers. Move them apart until there is a gap twice the length of the carton.

2. Tie a length of string from the top of one chair to the top of the other so that the string forms a shallow curve. This is one of the cables of the bridge.

3. Tie another string in the same way beside the first one. Then slide the strings as far apart as possible.

4. Now press down on the two strings. What happens to the chairs?

5. Can you use the bricks and more string to stop the chairs from caving in? The picture below might help you decide how to do this. Now push down on the strings again. Are the chairs stable now?

The bricks are the anchorages of the bridge. In real suspension bridges, the ends of the cables are anchored in huge concrete blocks that can withstand a pull of 10 161 t (10 000 tons) on the bridge.

Building the roadway

1. Cut off the long sides of the carton. Tape the sides together to make a roadway.

2. Trim the roadway so that it is as wide as the chairs.

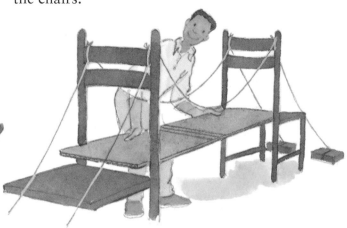

3. Lay the roadway on loops of string that hang from one cable to another. The strings holding the road should be taut. The roadway should be level with the chair seats, with its ends resting on the seats. Now check your bridge for strength in the next activity.

28

Is Your Suspension Bridge Wind-resistant?

Engineers test a model of a new bridge in a wind-tunnel to make sure the bridge will be safe in high winds. So put some toy cars or Plasticine balls on your bridge and test it for wind-resistance.

You'll need:
- a large fan
- your suspension bridge model
- a sheet of cardboard as large as the fan

1. Put the fan beside your bridge. Turn it to low, medium and high speeds. Do the changes in wind speed affect the strength of your bridge?

2. In addition to speed, winds can also have rhythm, or pulse. The pulse can be fast (at a high frequency) or slow (at a low frequency). To make the wind pulsate at a low frequency, hold the cardboard in front of the fan for two seconds, then remove it for two seconds, then put it in front of the fan, then remove it, and so on. Do this with each of the three wind speeds.

3. Now make the wind pulsate at a high frequency by moving the cardboard back and forth rapidly. Do this for each wind speed. Is your bridge strong? If not, how can you make it stronger? You might try adding more strings or some trusses along the sides of the roadway.

GALLOPING GERTIE

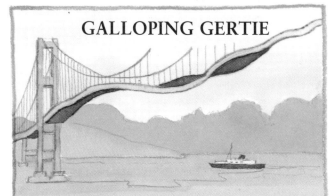

Driving across the Tacoma Narrows Bridge in Washington, U.S.A., used to be like riding a roller coaster. This suspension bridge was so flexible that the roadway moved up and down in waves as high as 1.5 m (5 feet) as traffic crossed it. That's why it was nicknamed Galloping Gertie.

Four months after the bridge was built, a steady wind destroyed it. Just as a swing in motion needs only small pushes to make it go higher and higher, the bridge's usual up and down movements became stronger and stronger when the wind pushed the bridge with the same rhythm. On the day the bridge collapsed, the roadway twisted and fell into the water below after only 70 minutes of steady blowing. Fortunately, no one was hurt.

What's at the Bottom of a Tower?

The two towers of a suspension bridge can be as tall as a 40-storey skyscraper. To support such tall towers, a strong foundation must be built at the bottom of the river or lake.

One way of creating a foundation is to build a giant hollow box called a cofferdam on the river bed. A special concrete that hardens underwater is poured down a tube into the cofferdam. Once the cofferdam is filled with hardened concrete, it is removed, and the tower is built on top of the concrete foundation.

Another method of building an underwater foundation involves air. A huge open-ended box as big as an ice-hockey rink is set on the river bed. This box is called a caisson. When air is pumped into the caisson, water is pushed out of it. This provides a watertight space where people can dig up mud and loose rock from the river bed. When very hard bedrock is reached, the caisson is filled with concrete. Then the tower is built on top of the caisson.

COFFERDAM

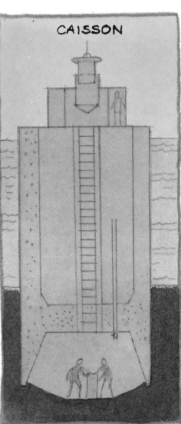

CAISSON

BRIDGE RECORDS

The world record for the longest suspension bridge is constantly being challenged. The Humber Estuary Bridge in England now holds the record with a span of 1410 m (4626 feet), but it will be surpassed in 1998 by the Akashi-Kaikyo Bridge linking the Japanese islands of Honshu and Shikoku. This bridge will have a main span of 1990 m (6529 feet), and its towers will be almost twice the height of the Humber Estuary Bridge towers.

BRIDGE ICES

Have you ever noticed signs warning of ice on bridges? Why doesn't ice form on both bridges *and* roads if they are in the same location? Heat from the earth warms roads, so they take a longer time to ice. Bridges have nothing to insulate them or to keep warmth in. They are exposed to the cold from the top, bottom and sides, so water turns easily to ice on bridges.

Bridging the Gap

Once the two towers of a suspension bridge are built, two long cables, or thick steel ropes, are strung from one tower to the other to hold the roadway. The workers who build these cables are among the bravest people in the world. Meet Joe; he's one of these cable workers.

Jan: What is the first step in building a cable, Joe?

Joe: We must get a rope across the water from one tower to the other. Usually, a boat pulls the rope across.

Jan: Then what do you do with the rope?

Joe: From the rope we hang a narrow platform called a catwalk hundreds of metres (yards) above the water. I stand on the catwalk and help build the cable.

Jan: How do you do that?

Joe: A cable is a strong rope made out of thousands of pencil-thick steel wires. A big wheel pulls the wires back and forth along the original rope. As the bundle of wires gets thicker, I make sure the wires lay evenly side by side. Once the bundle is thick enough, I wrap it up with more wire to make one thick cable.

Jan: How big is a cable?

Joe: In a very large suspension bridge, a cable can be as thick as four telephone poles in a bunch and as long as 1.6 km (1 mile).

Jan: You're certainly daring. Are the ends of the cables attached to the towers?

Joe: No. The cables go over the tops of the towers, and their ends are spread into enormous concrete blocks on either side of the river. These blocks are called anchorages.

Jan: What happens after the cables are built?

Joe: The roadway is hung from the cables by wires called hangers. Then the roadway is made stiff by adding trusses along the sides or by building box girders underneath.

The first bridge built over Capilano Canyon in British Columbia, Canada, made a laughing sound when it moved in the wind. People called it the Laughing Bridge. It was built out of rope by Native people and was as long as one-and-a-half soccer fields. Can you make a rope bridge strong enough to hold toy cars or Plasticine balls?

33

4. Moveable Bridges

Imagine that you are sailing down a river when you come to a bridge. The bridge is too low for your boat to pass under. What do you do? Simple! Move the bridge — or at least part of it.

There are five kinds of bridges that have moving parts. They open to let ships pass through a waterway and close to let traffic cross over them. Read on to find out about the different moveable bridges, and try making some of your own.

The pontoons of the Lake Washington Bridge are 18m (60 feet) wide and 6m (20 feet) deep. Inside are cables, water pumps and even catwalks for maintenance crews.

Pontoon Bridges

Pontoon bridges are built across lakes when the lake bottom is too soft to support piers A pontoon bridge floats with a roadway that rests on pontoons — huge concrete or metal boxes filled with air. Amazingly, some pontoons are as long as a football field and weigh about 4572 t (4500 tons) — and they still float! These pontoons are bolted together in a line and float on the water. When a boat needs to get from one part of a lake to another, one of the pontoons swings open like a gate.

The longest pontoon bridge in the world is the Second Lake Washington Bridge in Washington, U.S.A. It has 20 pontoons. What is the longest and strongest pontoon bridge you can build?

You'll need:
- 5 to 10 empty pop cans, all the same size
- packing tape
- rubber bands
- a bathtub of water
- manilla tagboard (3-ply Bristol board)
- Plasticine balls or toy cars

1. Cover the holes in the tops of the cans with tape.

2. Join together as many rubber bands as you have cans to make a chain. (To join one band to another, overlap the ends to make a small hole. Put the end of the bottom band through the hole and pull tightly.)

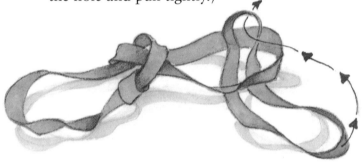

3. Put one pop can into each rubber band. If your pontoon bridge is long, use two parallel chains of rubber bands to link the cans. Real pontoons are joined end to end, but yours will be joined side by side.

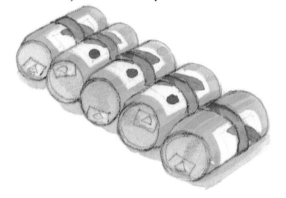

4. Float the cans, or pontoons, in the tub. Choose a beam from your engineering notes to use as a roadway along the top of the pontoons. Test your pontoon bridge for strength with Plasticine balls or toy cars.

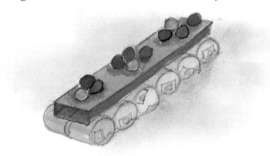

5. Can you design a pontoon bridge that swings open to let boats pass through? Try building your bridge in two sections with an extra rubber band to join the sections.

Engineering Problems
Does your pontoon bridge move around in the tub when you put cars on it? To prevent this from happening with real pontoon bridges, each pontoon is connected by cables to heavy concrete anchors buried in the bottom of the lake. How can you anchor your pontoon bridge in one spot? (Hint: Plasticine and string might help.)

Bascule Bridges

Y ou have probably read about bascule bridges in books or seen them in movies with medieval castles. They were called drawbridges in medieval times. A drawbridge spanned a moat that surrounded a castle and could be lifted up to stop enemies from entering the castle. Modern bascule bridges work in the same way. But instead of being raised to prevent enemies from crossing the river, the bascule bridge is raised to let boats past. A heavy weight operated by a small electric motor pushes down on one end of a span, or leaf. The other end lifts up like a see-saw and large boats pass through. When the leaf is lowered, cars can cross over the bridge. Some bridges have two spans that meet in the middle and lift up. They are called double-leaf bascule bridges. Try building a bascule bridge.

You'll need:
- scissors
- a cardboard carton
- a chair
- a nail
- thick string
- packing tape
- 2 bricks (or 2 heavy books)

1. Cut off one side of the carton. Trim along its length so that it is as wide as the chair seat.

2. With a nail, punch a hole near each corner at one end of the cardboard sheet.

3. Cut a length of string. Push one end of the string through one hole in the cardboard. Tie a large knot so that the string won't pull back through the hole.

4. Cut another length of string and do the same with the other hole.

5. Tape the other end of the cardboard to the back of the chair seat.

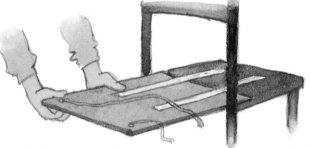

6. Run the strings over the back of the chair and tie each string to a brick. Can you figure out how to move the bricks so that the span will lift and lower?

To build a double-leaf bascule bridge, build another single-leaf span opposite the first one. Make sure the spans meet when they are lowered.

The two spans of a double-leaf bascule bridge are locked together where they meet. Can you design a lock for your double-leaf bridge so that traffic won't fall through the place where the spans meet? Try using a hole punch and some rubber bands.

Q. What is an artist's favourite kind of bridge?

A. A drawbridge.

CHOOSE YOUR OWN ADVENTURE

What would you do if you were driving across a double-leaf bascule bridge, and, just as you were approaching the middle, the two leaves of the bridge started to lift up? Sounds like something from an action movie, doesn't it? This actually happened to a bus driver on the Tower Bridge in London, England. The driver speeded up and the bus leaped over the widening gap. Is that what you would have done?

Swing Bridges

Engineers often build swing bridges near airports. Swing bridges have no towers or other high parts that could interfere with the flight paths of airplanes.

Swing bridges look like long beam bridges built close to the water. When a ship needs to pass through, the centre span of the bridge rotates, or turns, on its pier. The ship can then pass through either of the two channels formed on the sides of the pier.

Try building a swing bridge with Lego, Lasy or Tinker Toys. If you don't have these construction toys, use the materials listed on the next page.

You'll need:
- a thick nail
- a small margarine container and its lid
- a drinking straw
- a spool of thread
- scissors
- glue
- a manilla tagboard beam 15 cm x 45 cm (6 inches x 18 inches), chosen from your engineering notes on page 7

1. Use the nail to punch a hole in the middle of the bottom of the container.

2. Place the container upside down on the floor. Fit the straw through the hole so that one end touches the floor.

3. Put the other end of the straw through the hole in the spool and bring the spool down to rest on the container.

4. Cut off the part of the straw that sticks out above the spool.

5. Place the lid upside down on top of the spool. Glue the spool to the middle of the lid.

6. Glue the mid-point of the tagboard beam to the lid. To rotate the swing bridge, pull on the thread of the spool.

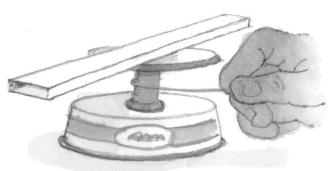

To use your bridge for traffic, build a road at either end of the rotating beam. You can build your road out of boxes, bricks, books, construction toys or whatever else you can imagine.

Vertical-Lift Bridges

A vertical-lift bridge works just as its name suggests. When a ship needs to pass through, the deck of the bridge lifts straight up, like an elevator. The deck is lifted up by cables and pulleys in a tower at each end of the deck.

An engineer might choose to build a vertical-lift bridge instead of another kind of moveable bridge because it is cheaper to build, uses little power to operate and moves as quickly as 15 m (50 feet) per minute.

If you have a Lego set with pulleys, you can use it to build a lift bridge. If not, build one with some simple materials.

You'll need:
- a metre (yard) stick
- 2 tables, desks or chairs
- 1 large nail
- 4 plastic lids from small yogurt containers
- scissors
- a drinking straw
- 2 pipe cleaners
- a side of a cardboard carton
- thick string
- 2 bricks (or 2 heavy books)

1. Lay the metre (yard) stick between two tables, desks or chairs that have a space between them.

2. To make a pulley, use the nail to punch a hole in the middle of two lids. Put the lids together and push a 5-cm (2-inch) piece of straw through the holes. Push a pipe cleaner through the straw and attach its ends to make a loop. Make another pulley the same way.

3. Hang the two pulleys from the metre (yard) stick by the pipe-cleaner loops.

4. Punch a hole near each corner of the cardboard.

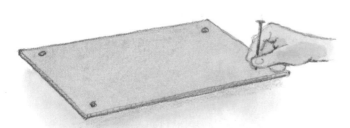

5. Cut two pieces of string a little longer than the width of the cardboard. Tie one string to each end of the cardboard as shown.

6. Tie a piece of string to the middle of each string at the ends of the cardboard.

7. Hang each string over a pulley. Use the bricks to raise the cardboard up to a level where you will build a road leading to and 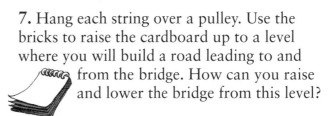 from the bridge. How can you raise and lower the bridge from this level?

Q. What kind of bridge do hitchhikers like?

A. A lift bridge.

41

Transporter Bridges

What if you needed to build a bridge where there was much more boat traffic than car and people traffic? You would probably build a transporter bridge. A transporter bridge is a huge platform that transports people and cars from one bank of a river to another. The platform hangs by strong wires from an overhead track that is attached to a tower on either side of the water.

Some transporter bridges can carry as many as six hundred passengers and nine cars across a river at one time.

A CROSS-OVER PUZZLE

A man has a hen, a fox and some corn. He must get them all across a bridge. But the bridge is so narrow and wobbly that he can only carry one thing at a time. How can he get them safely across without the hen eating the corn or the fox eating the hen? (See page 47 for the answer.)

Engineering Challenge

Now that you know how different kinds of bridges are built, why not get together with some friends and figure out how to make the strongest bridge possible. You can use Popsicle sticks, straws or even toothpicks and white glue. Any style of bridge will do, but try to make it long enough to span a gap of 40 cm (16 inches).

To test your bridge's strength, lay a broom handle or metre (yard) stick across your bridge. Hang a hook (made out of a hanger) from the rod and hang a bucket from the hook. How many cans of soup can you put into the bucket before your bridge collapses?

And Last but Not Least ...

Some large waterways are bridged by a combination of different kinds of bridges. The Chesapeake Bay Bridge in the U.S.A. has beam, cantilever and suspension parts. Combined with the two tunnels that join parts of the bridge together, the bridge is 28 km (17 1/2 miles) long.

THE ANTS GO MARCHING ...

When army ants look for food, the whole colony goes on a march. If they need to cross a tiny stream, some of the ants form a bridge by holding on to one another's legs. The bridge looks like a carpet made up of hundreds of ants.

Glossary

abutment: a concrete structure used for support at either end of a bridge

anchorage: a huge concrete block in which the ends of the cables of a suspension bridge are embedded

architect: a person who designs buildings

beam: long pieces of wood, concrete or steel that support the roadway of a bridge

cable: a flexible steel rope that supports the roadway of a suspension bridge

caisson: a watertight concrete box on the bottom of a river where people dig to reach bedrock (hard rock)

cofferdam: a large box or tube that stands on a river bed. It is filled with concrete to form the pier base for a bridge.

compression: the act of pressing down or squeezing together

deck: the roadway of a bridge

formwork: a mould into which concrete is poured to form a pier or beam

foundation: the supporting base of a bridge pier

keystone: a wedge-shaped stone at the top of an arch

leaf: the deck of a bascule bridge

pier: a column that connects the foundation to the deck of a bridge

pontoon: a concrete or metal box that floats and supports a pontoon bridge

reinforced concrete: concrete made stronger by steel rods or mesh

span: the part of a roadway that goes from one pier to another

strut: a bar that gives support or strength to a structure

tension: the act of pulling on the two ends of an object or stretching it

truss: a structure using triangular shapes to give strength to bridges

voussoir: a wedge-shaped stone used in building a stone arch

Answer A cross-over puzzle, p. 43:

The man takes the hen across and returns empty-handed.

Then he takes the fox across and returns with the hen.

Then he takes the corn across and returns empty-handed.

Finally he takes the hen across.

Index